WI

# WINNING AT WORK READINESS

## STEP-BY-STEP GUIDE TO

# INNOVATING AT SCHOOL & WORK

**Susan Burns Chong**

ROSEN
PUBLISHING®

New York

*This book is dedicated to Olivia and Caroline, two very creative, caring, and amazing girls.*

Published in 2015 by The Rosen Publishing Group, Inc.
29 East 21st Street, New York, NY 10010

## Library of Congress Cataloging-in-Publication Data

Chong, Susan Burns.
Step-by-step guide to innovating at school & work/Susan Burns Chong.—First edition.
    pages cm.—(Winning at work readiness)
Includes bibliographical references and index.
Audience: Grades 7–12.
ISBN 978-1-4777-7786-2 (library bound)—ISBN 978-1-4777-7788-6 (pbk.)—ISBN 978-1-4777-7789-3 (6-pack)
1. Technological innovations—Juvenile literature. 2. Inventions—Juvenile literature. 3. Creative ability—Juvenile literature. I. Title.
HC79.T4C478 2015
650.1—dc23

2014003044

*Manufactured in the United States of America*

# CONTENTS

# INTRODUCTION

At the heart of any innovation is the inspiration. This inspiration may be a problem, a challenge, or an opportunity. For siblings Simone and Jake Bernstein, seventeen and fifteen respectively, theirs was a frustration. They had hoped to volunteer their time in St. Louis, Missouri, but had no central resource for learning about volunteer opportunities. So, they decided to innovate. They worked all summer to create volunTEENnation.org, and now, about 7,500 young people have used the site to give back to their communities.

The Bernstein siblings have gained notoriety by creating their website and have become vocal supporters of teen innovators. Jake was recently quoted in the Clayton–Richmond Heights Patch, saying, "We are generation on, ready to take action, and dive into solving problems in the community." He stated further, "We have duties as citizens in the world. Some of them start before 18-years-old." Innovators see something hopeful and possible in their inspirations.

Today's middle school and high school students are equipped to innovate. According to a current study of teens' access to technology by the Pew Internet and American Life Project, 95 percent of teens in the United States, ages twelve to seventeen, are online several times a day to a few times a month. With ideas and resources available from around the world and from throughout history, accessible with the Internet on multiple devices at any moment, information can be shared.

Young people can learn quickly about community issues, national and international crises, and global needs. For the first time ever, students can respond immediately, through action and through words, on sites like Facebook, Twitter, Thunderclap, YouTube, and Instagram. Teens have the capability to get in-depth analysis of issues, to raise awareness, and to make connections. Now more than ever, teens are ready to impact the world. They are ready to innovate.

Young people can organize efforts to address social, political, and environmental issues. Here, teen volunteers in Miami Beach, Florida, are working to clean up a local beach.

# Chapter 1

# PREPARE YOURSELF

K urt Andres is a high school student in Tucson, Arizona. According to the website Innovation Generation, a youth-created site celebrating young innovators, Kurt recently created a complicated tool. It measures any dynamic imbalance in the propellers of wind turbines. The tool records valuable information about the way turbines are working. Engineers are able to make them more efficient and safe and less prone to damage. Kurt's innovative project has impacted the field of energy efficiency.

Before inventing this tool, Kurt was curious about the wind turbines in his town. He wondered about them. He observed a challenge and came up with a solution! What was happening in his brain when he got his great idea? How did he come to this innovative answer?

## A LITTLE BRAIN SCIENCE

Scientists have been working to unlock the mysteries of the human brain for a long time. With new technology, like MRIs and CAT scans, scientists have recently made new discoveries about the brain, especially about the adolescent brain. This is a brief summary of the brain's geography.

The best place to begin in the brain is the nerve cell, or neuron. Neurons are the tools that the brain uses to receive and communicate information. The average brain holds ten billion to one hundred billion neurons. Information travels as electric pulses from the cell body and down its cable-like axon. The

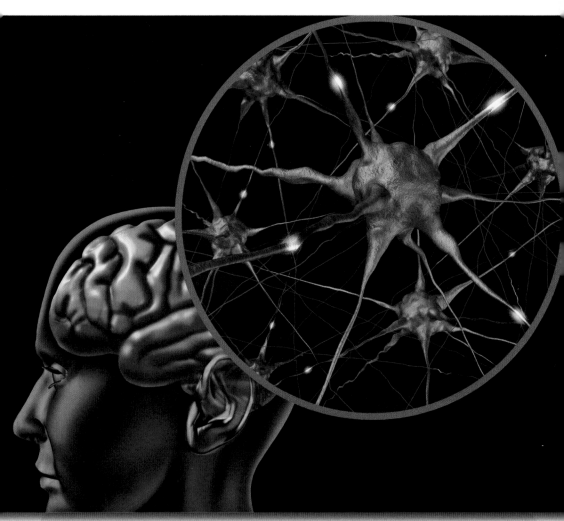

"Neuroplasticity" is a term researchers use to describe the brain's ability to change. Learning or memorizing new information can actually reorganize the pathways or connections in our brains.

information passes through synapses, or gaps, between neurons and connects with the new neuron's dendrites, long feathery branches that receive information. Connections are formed. Scientists often think of these new pathways as creating a "neural forest." This forest becomes denser with more learning. For the most part, these neurons are layered together, covering the brain in what is called the cerebral cortex.

The cerebral cortex covers the two halves of the brain—the right hemisphere and the left hemisphere. These halves have different roles. The right hemisphere is in charge of things such as face recognition, sense of direction, concrete thinking, nonverbal memory, and musical patterns. The left hemisphere is the center of letters, words, and language; abstract thinking; verbal memory; logical problem solving; and math.

People used to believe that creative thoughts emerged only from the right brain. Scientists know differently, now. Creative thinking happens in several places in the brain. The front and sides of the cortex, also called the prefrontal cortex, are in charge of executive functioning. This means that this area of the brain is involved in planning, decision making, and reasoning. This area is crucial for exploring and fact finding. In the middle of the prefrontal cortex is the area that helps with self-reflection, compassion, and life memory. This area is active when daydreaming or imagining. Each part works with the others to create an idea.

Now that we have looked at the actual brain, let's explore how to use it.

## TRAIN YOUR BRAIN

People have habits, or ways of doing things, that are particular to them. For example, one person might always put on her left shoe first, while another might put on his right. A person might say "umm" when he is talking and thinking at the same time. Another

# THREE TYPES OF INNOVATORS

Stories in the news and online will likely highlight three different kinds of innovation—social, disruptive, and entrepreneurial. As you hear about innovators, try to figure out which description fits for each.

The social innovator is someone who creates a change in systems or services, such as Jane Addams, pioneering social worker, or Dolores Huerta, Latina community organizer. The Bernstein siblings from the beginning of this book are social innovators. They created a new resource for potential teen volunteers. When they created their volunteer website, they changed the way that young people engage with their communities.

A disruptive innovator is one who significantly challenges and changes the way that people behave. Martin Luther King Jr., Nelson Mandela, and Mahatma Gandhi are great examples. Each one challenged society to move away from discrimination in creative ways. Their influence forever changed the world.

An entrepreneurial innovator is someone who offers a new business or product. The creation of it must significantly shift the way people interact. Steve Jobs of Apple, Inc. created the iPad, iPhone, and iTunes and transformed communication, education, and entertainment. Jerry Yang, cofounder of Yahoo!, introduced a different way to find information. The new emphasis on the creation of apps for devices has opened the way for students as young as elementary school to become entrepreneurial innovators.

might twirl her hair. Habits are the behaviors that people have practiced over a lifetime.

Researchers are studying a new kind of habit—a "habit of mind." The idea is that just as we always do certain things, we also think certain things. These habits of thinking are very powerful. They affect behavior.

Many researchers and authors are studying successful teens and what helps them to be successful. Are they successful naturally? Not necessarily. According to Tony Wagner's book *Creating Innovators*, people can learn to become successful by practicing healthy habits of mind. Curiosity, collaboration, connection, and action are necessary habits for innovation.

To explain further, innovative teens practice asking questions and wondering about things until a new habit of mind is created—curiosity. In the same way, teens practice working together for a habit of collaboration. Making associations between information learned or experienced fosters a habit of creating connections. Doing something when the moment is right creates a habit of taking action.

Researchers also write about the importance of another powerful habit—empathy. Empathy is the capacity to imagine how someone else experiences a situation. When innovators can envision being the person using the technology, service, or product, they are more likely to create an effective solution. The stories of the struggles and frustrations that people endure can inspire and motivate good ideas. Innovators practice understanding the situations of others and become empathic.

# GROWTH MIND-SET

Researcher Paul Tough proposes that students generally have two ways of thinking about themselves academically—as either smart/not smart or as learners. The students who see themselves as "good at math" or "bad at spelling" possess what is called a set mind-set. They

Student innovators in Modesto, California, make final adjustments to their robot, which is designed to pick up small objects. They are thinking with a growth mind-set.

are less likely to have confidence when trying a new skill in a less-favored subject. The students who see themselves as learners have what is called a growth mind-set. These students are more likely to take risks and to try new subjects. They have more confidence when facing a challenge. They understand that the brain is growing with each idea, whether it is a success or a failure. They are innovators!

## BEGINNER'S MIND

"Beginner's mind" is practiced by Buddhists and others who meditate. The term describes the concept of looking at a situation

11

# DESIGN CHALLENGES

In your school, you have probably been asked to work on a design challenge. A design challenge is a problem that needs a creative answer. The solutions come only with collaborative problem solving and by following certain steps together. Students get to apply what they are learning at their desks to a real life situation.

For example, to help students learn to think and act together, a teacher might ask them to do a warm-up design challenge. The challenge might be to build a structure using random items, such as spaghetti and marshmallows. It seems impossible, but by following the process, the group will learn important lessons. Even if the structure fails, they will have found out important information about themselves and the process.

Design challenges may also have connections to the real world on a larger scale. For example, schools might want to redesign their schedule of classes or their disciplinary practices. They might want to address bullying or relationship violence. The town library may need to figure out how to engage more young people. A community may need to address hunger or homelessness. The real world problems, challenges, and opportunities are abundant.

Organizations and large companies are beginning to recognize that teens have infinite capacity for coming up with innovative ideas. They are beginning to host competitions for teens to solve their most challenging issues. These contests often come with prestige, scholarships, or cash prizes. You will hear about some of these in the text, and additional resources appear at the end of this book.

with great curiosity and with little judgment, just as a child would. Have you ever watched a baby pick up a new toy? The baby will seem to stare at the toy, throw it, bang it, and likely put it in her mouth. She is exploring the toy with pure curiosity. Someone practicing beginner's mind is more likely to ask questions and to explore an idea to its depths—without doubts.

Having a beginner's mind takes practice. Even by middle school and high school, students are taught to make quick judgments. They are praised when they have all the answers. Students can discipline their minds by observing their thoughts when

By practicing "beginner's mind," young people see new connections and possibilities. This open thinking leads to innovative solutions to local, state, national, and international problems.

thinking of or discussing new ideas. Sometimes, students will hear about a new idea and think, "It will never work!" or "Sounds good, but..." or "I don't think this is a good idea." These thoughts can dismiss a good possibility too early in the discussion. Sometimes, students with closed-minded thinking have not gathered all the important information yet.

With beginner's mind, students practice thinking differently. They practice having an open mind. Innovators often use the phrase, "Yes, and..." to move ideas forward. When they hear about a new idea, they keep their thoughts on all the possibilities. They look for connections and opportunities.

Many people write and think about beginner's mind. According to Zen teacher Shunryu Suzuki, "In the beginner's mind there are many possibilities, in the expert's there are few." True innovators practice thinking with a beginner's mind.

# Chapter 2

# INVESTIGATE

George Washington Carver, Thomas Edison, and Beulah Louise Henry were three of the United States' early, most innovative thinkers. When faced with problems, they examined the challenges in great detail and ended up finding hundreds of innovative solutions.

Farmers during the turn of the nineteenth century struggled to grow crops. George Washington Carver taught farmers crop rotation, a practice to enrich the soil with nutrient-rich crops. Then, during World War I, resources were scarce. Carver looked at what was in abundance in his area—peanuts, sweet potatoes, and pecans. He created hundreds of ways to use these crops. He invented more than 300 peanut-based products, including soaps, ink, and milk. Using sweet potatoes, he invented 115 products, including artificial rubber. He invented 75 products using pecans, too.

Thomas Alva Edison held 1,093 patents. His innovations and improvements still impact many parts of life, including telecommunications, electricity, movies and sound, mining, and construction. He is recognized for starting what we now call a research laboratory. He brought many brilliant inventors to his lab to help create innovations.

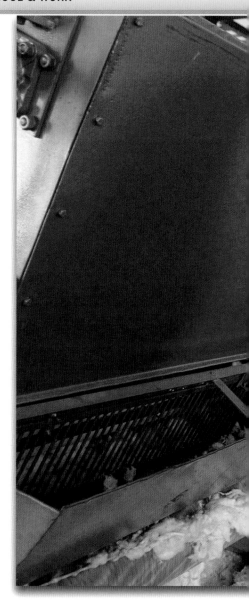

Beulah Louise Henry patented 49 different inventions. She is famous for more than 100 new ideas. Her innovations were designed to make home life easier. Henry invented a vacuum-sealed ice-cream freezer, a doll with changing eye color, and an improvement to the sewing machine. According to Invent.org, when she thought of an innovative idea, "she had a complete picture of each finished product in her mind." She would articulate her vision and then a model would be created using her explanation. In the 1920s, her prolific inventions earned her the nickname "Lady Edison."

Since you have chosen to read this guide, you must have something in your life that frustrates, challenges, inspires, or intrigues you. Great! This is the first step. Now, let's add your name to the list of famous innovators.

# DESIGN IT

Design thinking is the process of innovating. The first step for students is to define the problem, challenge, or inspiration. Next, students research the issue. Then, using beginner's mind, they generate ideas to address the problem. Once they have identified possible solutions, they prototype their ideas. This process may continue as students learn from

"Fair trade" is an innovative idea that focuses on people. This means that local producers, like this cotton spinning factory in Indore, India, are given a fair price for their products.

testing their ideas. In innovation, students use empathy to imagine the experience of the users, and they use this information to guide the design.

Innovators need to think about their problem, challenge, or opportunity. They think about what they already know. Then, they get it all down. Some use a computer to create a document; others use software to map it out graphically. Some use a pen and paper and write it all down. Some innovators use large paper and markers to record everything they know.

By looking at this knowledge, innovators think about the facts that they do not know and the facts that they need to find out. Soon, they come up with questions that they need to answer. Innovators write down the questions that make them wonder. These questions might look like this: "What is the number of..." or "What happens when...?" or "How does this work?"

## RESEARCH IT

Innovators use the lists of information and questions to research the problem, challenge, or opportunity. They take time to figure out what they want to learn. Innovators usually head straight for the library to find out more. (This is probably how you found this book!) This inquiry may lead to additional research through books, magazines, and Internet sites. Innovators can find answers to their questions and may even find inspiration.

Sometimes innovators need to jump right into the situation. Observation, interviews, and analogous research are three common ways to find answers.

If the problem is in a school, workplace, neighborhood, or other place, innovators spend time there, recording what happens. They observe the people and what they are doing. They take notes about the furniture, equipment, lighting, and arrangement in the space. Innovators give special attention to the way things work. They write down their observations about how people and things interact. This is important information.

When researching an idea, plan ahead! Bring your technology, notebook, and pen to the library to help you as you gather information. Folders and binders help organize your work, too.

Innovators may also learn a lot about their problem, challenge, or opportunity by talking with people. They brainstorm a list of people in school, work, or the neighborhood who have experience or who might be interested in the project. Innovators often use the project to meet outrageously interesting people, such as artists, musicians, celebrities, authors, politicians, and other famous people.

Innovators know how to set up interviews. They contact the person or group to set a date and time to meet. Meetings may take place using the phone or web conferencing. If an interview takes place in person, innovators choose a public place, like a library or

# FAIL PROUD!

As a young innovator, you are certain to face failure as you move through the stages of innovation. You might feel embarrassment as critics (friends, family, or teachers) observe your attempts. They may try to dissuade you from moving forward. You might even feel like giving up. To stay on track, try remembering that through failure, great ideas may emerge.

Many people who are now famous in science, politics, sports, movies, and the arts also experienced significant failures. For example, before becoming the sixteenth president, Abraham Lincoln failed as a businessman, and he lost numerous political elections. He went on to preside during an incredibly important time in the United States. Walt Disney was fired from his job and became bankrupt from failed businesses. He kept trying and eventually founded the successful Disney Company. Michael Jordan, considered by many to be the greatest basketball player in the history of the game, was cut from his own high school's basketball team. He never gave up, winning six NBA championships. Vera Wang, the now famous fashion designer, failed to make the Olympic figure skating team. Dismayed, she turned to a different profession—fashion magazine editor. When she did not get a promotion, she left to become a world-class fashion designer.

Innovators say, "Fail proud!" This mantra keeps them focused on their goal. When you have the courage to keep trying, the outcome may very well be true learning, fame and fortune, or making the world a better place.

restaurant, and they always bring along a friend. Innovators write down questions ahead of time and bring a notebook and pen or a device to take notes.

## THINK OUTSIDE THE BOX

Analogous research is another way to learn about the problem. Innovators use new situations that are similar to the problem to find insights into the challenge, opportunity, or need. For example, a group at a school would like to figure out a better way to move students through the busy hallways. They need to make sure that everyone arrives on time and without students running into each other. For their analogous research, they would visit a busy airport. At the airport, they would observe how passengers move through the terminal without trouble. They would observe the patterns and even talk to people about their experiences walking in the airport.

This research phase is important and can often be overwhelming. Innovators reflect on what they have learned. After each research session, observation, interview, or analogous research visit, they must write down their insights. Many students choose to write their reflections on sticky notes. These moveable notes allow groups to organize their thoughts during meetings.

While researching, students may discover new information that they want to explore further. If their plan is clear enough, going down these "rabbit holes" won't get them off track. On the contrary, it can lead to important discoveries. Innovators are open to new ideas but are careful to avoid distraction.

## PARTNER UP

The most progressive innovators surround themselves with peers who share their mind-set, energy, and ideas. Much like creating a

Can you think of adults in your school or workplace who might help your innovation team? Adult partners share ideas, find resources, and teach others from their own perspectives.

presidential cabinet, innovators invite people with specific talents, skills, and experiences to join them in the work. In fact, many organizations and businesses now encourage their employees to work collaboratively.

Young innovators seek out adults in their schools, community centers, after-school programs, sports teams, and other settings to help them. Adults who can teach, mentor, guide, and partner with teens can be very helpful to the innovation. The adults may also have connections to organizations and groups that bring resources. The resources may include funding, space, supplies, or expertise, and they can become beneficial parts of the partnership.

Learning about a problem, opportunity, or challenge from different viewpoints may be very helpful, too. One innovator participating in an effort to end violence in schools in Philadelphia agrees with the importance of working with peers and adults. Shania Morris, a ninth grader, recently talked with the *Notebook*, the independent newsletter for the school district. She said, "After I joined [the group], I became a more critical thinker. I started thinking about my school and my education from a more 'big picture' perspective. Now I am more aware of why some students act out, why teachers teach the way they do…. I under-stand what causes some of the dynamics in my school more than I did before."

# Chapter 3

# IMAGINE

$S$ix girls from Ames, Iowa, were recently awarded a FIRST LEGO League Global Innovation Award. For their project, they created a prosthetic tool that would help people who are unable to grasp a writing utensil. These young innovators researched artificial limbs and met a girl struggling with her disability. They learned that she was unable to write because of missing fingers on her hand. The six listened, shared, and set out to create a tool that would help her to write. And they did it.

You have now moved through the investigative phase, and you are ready to imagine. Use the research you have gathered and rely on your team of collaborators. Dreaming big with your idea is OK, but following a structured process may lead you to more success.

## GETTING ORGANIZED

This phase is the most exciting part of the innovation process, but it can also be the most confusing. Students meet with their teams to share their research and in the process, organize it. As innovators talk and listen together, they follow this guide:

❯ Share the knowledge
❯ Find themes
❯ Discover new insights
❯ Ask questions
❯ Brainstorm

Innovators often end up with tall piles of sticky notes and huge posters from their discussions with their team. If they need to take a break in the process, they always take notes on what they

As the facilitator of this innovative process, you may need to bring many blank sticky notes to meetings. As a team, you will be able to move ideas around, grouping them into new themes or insights.

have discussed so far. Taking a photo of the sticky notes in their theme groupings can be helpful, too.

Innovators encourage some general guidelines before beginning these sessions. The facilitator asks the group, "What ground

# MEETING EXPECTATIONS

Now that you've pulled your team together, you'll need to make sure that meetings go well. The person who makes meetings go smoothly is called a facilitator. The skills the facilitator has are called facilitation skills. Here are a few tips to strengthen your facilitation skills.

Invite the peers and adults who you think would contribute to the sessions. Make sure they know the time and location of the meeting. Plan your meetings. Create a list of what you want to cover and how long you want to talk about each item on your list. Share this agenda with participants ahead of time. Have all of the supplies that you'll need— sticky notes, poster paper, pens, markers, crayons, handouts, and computers. The list goes on. Teams also appreciate healthy snacks during the meetings. (Remember to check first to see if you are able to eat in the meeting location.)

The facilitator is also in charge of keeping the work moving forward. Sometimes participants can talk too much or get off track. Make sure that your meetings are positive and productive. Talk to your team about the importance of listening to each other. If people are getting frustrated, change your agenda or switch to a new "How might we...?" question. You can always invite new people into the conversation if your team seems stuck.

rules will help us work together best?" The group may agree on rules such as "Nothing is impossible," "No judgment," and "One person talks at a time." The group may also agree to practice beginner's mind. As innovators listen to the team's ideas, they remember not to think or say things that could tamp down the spirit of innovation, such as, "Sounds good, but...", or "No, that will never work!"

# SHARING THE KNOWLEDGE

To begin the process, the innovator and the team remember and write down important information from the research phase. Using sticky notes, they write all of the details that they learned during their reading, observations, interviews, or analogous research. Even if a team member has pages of notes from an interview, she will need to find the most critical pieces of information. These get written on sticky notes. This is the information to be shared with the group.

For example, the shared knowledge of the group studying the flow of students in the hallway might look like this: From the library research, an innovator could write, "Nationally, students need an average of three minutes at their lockers to get what they need for their next class." Shared knowledge from the observations might read, "Students crash into each other when rushing to class," or "noisy lockers" or "teachers and students arrive after the bell." The knowledge from the interviews could be written as, "Our principal reports several injuries." They could include information from their analogous research at the airport, as well. "Travelers like fast-paced music" or "Directions are clearly marked."

Once all the members of the group have written their knowledge on their own sticky notes, this information may be shared. The facilitator prepares a white board, flip chart paper, or a wall

with space to post the notes. After every person has a chance to share and post, the innovator and the team move on to discussing themes.

## FINDING THEMES

Themes are found by grouping similar ideas together. Innovators look at the shared knowledge and group ideas by a topic that connects them. For example, back to the school example, the group might find that many of the ideas shared involve similar topics. Thoughts regarding students, teachers, timing, or hallway complaints may repeat. These become the themes.

As the group decides the themes, the facilitator writes them on the board, flip-chart paper, or wall. The team members move the sticky notes around until they are placed under the appropriate theme. This part may create lively conversation. Team members may agree and disagree on themes or placement of the sticky notes. Facilitators understand that this stage can be flexible and that multiple arrangements are possible.

## DISCOVERING INSIGHTS

Now the group can stand back and look at the process. The next step is to discover the wisdom or insights from the research. Once

Brainstorming is a process that innovators use to gather ideas from the team. Remember to practice beginner's mind in your discussions, thinking openly about ideas and looking for connections.

all of the knowledge is grouped by theme, innovators take time to read through all the sticky notes. They reflect on the themes and try to make connections.

In this step, the team talks about or writes down all of the thoughts they have about the information and its themes. They explore the problem and why the different parts of the issue are challenging. For example, "Lockers are a challenge because they are too rusty to open and too small to store technology safely." Facilitators ensure that all ideas are posted and the group is thinking with beginner's mind. Through this process, innovators and their teams become ready to move to the next step.

## ASKING QUESTIONS

The innovator and the team members now look at the insights with curiosity. The group may start with one insight statement. They craft questions to address the idea that they discovered about the problem or opportunity. The questions should be designed to spark ideas immediately. They should also guide the group's future steps.

For example, again using the hallway example, a student innovator might choose the insight statement about the small, rusty lockers. The innovator might ask, "How can we improve the lockers so that students don't struggle and have more time?" Or the innovator might ask, "How could we design an alternative storage for technology?" No question is incorrect. Each one may lead to an innovation.

## BRAINSTORMING

The next step is to think of and write down all of the ideas that could answer the "How might we...?" questions. The ideas can be simple or complicated, crazy or reasonable. Brainstorming sessions are no place for judgment. There is no limit to the ideas. The more the better.

When innovators ask big questions, big results are likely to happen. Matthew Charchenko's story is a great example.

According to the *Redmond Report* newspaper, Matthew, fourteen, has always been interested in the weather. When he began to ask deeper questions about the reliability of making predictions about weather, he likely asked, "How can we develop a better way to predict weather by sharing what we learn?" He and a friend from Pennsylvania formed a U.S.-based group,

Matthew Charchenko's questions about weather resulted in the formation of a weather-predicting organization.

GeoEnvironmental Atmosphere (GEA). This organization focuses on bringing the geo-environmental and atmospheric sciences together to make the best weather predictions.

After the brainstorming session, the final step is to look at all the ideas and to choose one to try. This choice may be something simple or something huge. For Matthew Charchenko, the answer was to create a new national organization. The innovator and the team may find the answer clear, or the group may need to vote. If the group cannot decide on just one, innovators will help the group decide on the top two or three ideas. The ideas they select should be able to be accomplished.

# Chapter 4

# INNOVATE

N ow is the time to put your idea to the test. When innovators are ready to try their ideas, they create a prototype. A prototype is a model. Innovators use the model to make the idea better. This process can be both fun and frustrating, so innovators need to be focused on what they want the prototype to teach them about their idea.

## HOW DOES A PROTOTYPE WORK?

Justin Krell, sixteen, from Plankinton, South Dakota, is a great example of someone using the prototype process. He recently competed at the Intel International Science and Engineering Fair with his prototype, HardHit. The HardHit device records data in a car crash. The data would help doctors know how a person's head moved during the crash. Doctors could more quickly determine if the patient has a serious head injury and how to treat it.

According to an article on Mashables.com, Justin thought of the invention when he was playing football. He imagined the tackles. He then thought of the collisions that passengers in a car endure.

When Justin Krell prototyped the HardHit device, he continued to ask questions and explore possibilities. When your team prototypes, be sure to take good notes on how the innovation works.

The device fits inside a car seat, and currently the data is stored on a memory card. After trying his prototype in test rigs, Justin thought of two ways to improve it. He is working to change how quickly the information can be accessed. He would like the device to be able to text the information to the medics at the scene of the accident. He would also like to program the device so that it accounts for susceptibility to head injury (for example, previous head trauma) for each passenger in the car. Justin took his idea, designed it, created a prototype, tested it, and then evaluated how it performed.

Students at a school in Chicago, Illinois, work together to design a prototype as part of an engineering workshop. What would your team like to learn about your innovation?

## PROTOTYPING

Importantly, prototypes must be broken down into smaller parts. In this way, innovators can really learn about their idea. By examining each step of the design, innovators can see where the prototype fails or succeeds. Most innovators map out each step of the design. They might decide to prototype only one part of the design at a time.

Before creating a prototype, innovators think about, write down, and share what they hope to learn through the process. The facilitator and the group agree on specific questions that they have

# TAKING ACTION

In her granddaughter's biography of her life, Madame C. J. Walker is described as an entrepreneurial innovator. Walker was the first woman in America to become a self-made millionaire. She achieved this by designing and prototyping hair-care products for African American women. In the late 1800s, stores did not offer these products. She created her own. It wasn't easy. She prototyped and tested until she was confident that she could sell her own line of beauty products. She expanded throughout the country, adding beauty schools that taught people how to use her products. She met a need with great innovation and grew her business. Walker was bold and creative, especially at a time when there was great racial discrimination. She found a need and discovered a solution.

Truthfully, many people have great ideas. The ideas that become successful are the ones that are brought to life. The innovators, like Walker, are fearless and determined. Every great idea begins with someone taking the first step. This first step might be telling a friend or posting a thought or writing an article. Sometimes fear can get in the way. Fear of failure and fear of success can be very powerful. Taking that first step can seem really intimidating.

Innovators find creative ways to feel bold enough to do something about their ideas. You might keep a journal, have a mentor, or set goals with timelines. You might plan celebrations and rewards through the process. You may need to decide how you will be courageous enough to take that first step.

about the prototype. These might be mechanical or physical, addressing how the prototype functions. These questions could also address the experience of the innovation from another person's perspective. This strengthens empathy, a critical component of design thinking.

Innovating can be a messy process! Remember that if your idea fails, you can still learn valuable information. If your idea succeeds, you can continue to make it better.

## MODELS

Next, a model is created. This prototype could include one part of the solution or every part, from customer need to satisfaction with the service to access of the product. The prototype process brings to life the imaginative ideas of the innovators.

Innovators prototype their ideas in a variety of ways. They may build a working model like the HardHit device that Justin Krell created. They may choose to produce their ideas using 3-D modeling software. More simply, innovators may create pictures, diagrams, or posters to represent it. A fun and helpful exercise may be to use video, photos, or art to create a commercial for the product. If they are working on an innovative new service, innovators may try out the idea using role-plays or storytelling.

Innovators recognize that this stage of the process will teach them about the changes they will need to make to improve their idea. This phase is not about success. It is more about failure and discovery.

## DEBRIEF

After the prototype testing, innovators generally discuss a few critical questions, such as what happened, what worked, what could have been better, and what happened that was a surprise.

Innovators gather feedback from various sources that may have been impacted by the prototype. If the test run happened at work, then customers, coworkers, or work supervisors may weigh in. If the prototype was tested in a school, then members of that community would give feedback to help answer these questions. Peers, teachers, staff, and administration may all give comments about the idea. For the group working on the hallway issue, for example, students and teachers using the new idea could give feedback.

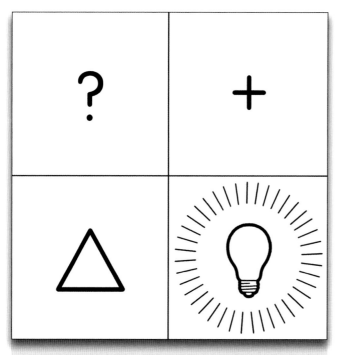

Using this helpful diagram as a guide, your team may record what happened (?), what worked (+), what could have been different (Δ), and what was learned (lightbulb).

Sometimes giving and getting feedback can be difficult. When talking about the prototype, group facilitators suggest setting a rule for the conversation. When people are giving feedback, they could use the phrases, "I like...," "I wish...," and "What if...?" So for example, a student could say, "I like the size of the new lockers. I wish I could utilize the space better. What if students could design shelving for each locker?" The facilitator then records these answers.

Innovators may iterate or repeat the prototype if they have time. Through this repeated testing, innovators can learn about the technical working of the idea. Iterating might also educate innovators about the user's experience. The information learned may lead to even more specific improvements.

# Chapter 5

# KEEP LEARNING

Greyson McCluskey, sixteen, from Indian Trail, North Carolina, won a contest from Fahrenheit 212, an innovation firm. According to Entrepreneur.com, he won the "Wouldn't It Be Cool If" contest with his great idea. Greyson designed a tool called the Baby Safe Rider. His idea was an alert system to protect babies from dangerous outcomes if accidentally left in a hot car. Greyson was invited to work with the company over a year's time to develop his business plan. "From now on, we'll be working with more details, focusing on sparking the interest of investors and people that want to get involved with this," said Greyson in the online article after winning the prize.

Now that your prototype has been tested, you have critical decisions to make and actions to take. You must figure out what to learn from what you have tested and what to do about it.

## CREATE A PLAN

At this stage, innovators create a plan to guide their ideas. To do this, they must describe how the idea will work. Innovators may make calculated predictions about a few critical parts of their

Imagine! Your innovation could actually save lives. Be sure to think about your idea from another person's perspective and to predict what his or her experience will be like.

solution. Innovators think about their customers, or users of the product, service, or outcome. They figure out the offer, or what the customers will be getting. They research sources of revenue, or money coming into the project. Innovators also imagine touch points, or times when people will come in contact with the idea.

A business plan is helpful to the next phase of piloting the idea. Most innovators need business advice when creating a business plan. Team members may be able to help. Members of the community may contribute wisdom, too. The Service Corps of Retired Executives (SCORE) is a great resource for young innovators. This national organization is made of working and retired professionals who volunteer to help innovators with every step of an idea. The volunteers mentor, teach, and provide educational information. SCORE has offices all over the country. It even has a youth-specific website.

## DESIGN THE PILOT

In the prototyping stage, innovators test one or two specific parts of the idea. During the pilot stage of the project, innovators create their full idea, but on a smaller scale. The goal of the pilot is to see if the idea would work in the real world.

Before piloting the idea, innovators may work in the team to think about a few important details. They are encouraged to ask questions about pricing, payment, customer experience, and other aspects of the project. For example, should people pay for the idea? What are people willing to pay for this service or product? What amounts are other businesses charging? Are there incentives that customers earn to keep them coming back? What are additional ways that customers will come in contact with the idea? Innovators even need to explore how the project supports its employees or volunteers. Once the innovator and the team come up with the questions they want to answer, they can begin the pilot test.

Remember the example with the students and their hallway issue? If the team chose to pilot test a new locker design, they would start with a few students but not the entire school. If they chose to create new traffic patterns in the hallway, they might begin with one class. This stage is about getting answers to the questions before involving too many people and too many resources.

## GET READY TO LAUNCH

Throughout this process, innovators think about the partners, materials, and resources that will help them make their idea work.

In school, these partners might be teachers, principals, coaches, group leaders, parents, or volunteers. In the workplace or neighborhood, team members may include coworkers, supervisors, mentors, or local experts. Innovators know that in every community, people with experience and expertise are willing to help share their knowledge.

Importantly, innovators understand that a team must be managed. Setting the roles and responsibilities within a team is critical. Innovators guide team members to know the expectations they face as members of the project.

Business plans can be complicated. Find someone in your school, workplace, or community who can help you create a plan to successfully launch your idea.

When innovators think about materials, they predict the kinds of technology, equipment, and supplies they will need to implement the idea. Most of the innovators included in this book needed to borrow time in a lab or find recycled supplies for their prototypes. At this point, innovators need to think long term about their resources.

# FIND THE MONEY

When it is time to pilot the idea or launch the business plan, innovators need money. Innovators can hold a traditional school fund-raiser like a bake sale or catalog sale, public performance, or donation jar collection. Sometimes innovators let family or friends know about their idea. When reaching out, they make a personal request. Phone calls, e-mail blasts, or letters can also be effective.

Grants may be a source of funding. Many local, state, and national foundations or companies seek to fund smaller creative projects. Innovators can research them online or visit a local philanthropy center. Innovators know that grant writing can be challenging. They often enlist the help of a good writer when applying for grants.

The Internet has brought a new kind of fund-raising. Crowdfunding websites build on a traditional fund-raising strategy. Historically, creative people, like artists, musicians, or writers, may have been funded by patrons or backers. These supporters offered money so that the creators could keep working on their creative efforts.

Raising money for innovations has become easier through the Internet. The cofounder of Indiegogo, Danae Ringelmann, shares her story about the crowdfunding site.

With the Internet, finding people to become backers is easier. Websites like Kickstarter, Indiegogo, Rockethub, appbackr, and Quirky offer innovators an opportunity to raise awareness about and money for special efforts. Even teen innovators are participating in the creation of these crowd-funding tools. Jared Kleinert, seventeen, from Boca Raton, Florida, recently launched Synergist, a site for funding social innovation projects.

On the sites, innovators prepare a creative plea to ask for money, through video, music, or written word. They also predict how much money they will need to raise. Visitors to the site read about the project. If they like it, they may pledge money to support it. Reaching a goal may require many small donations. When the asking amount is achieved, the money is released and the project can begin.

Kickstarter is likely the best-known crowdfunding site. According to the Kickstarter website, 5.4 million people have pledged over $900 million and have funded 53,000 creative projects since 2009. Projects are posted every day.

## GET THE WORD OUT

Once the team has prototyped, created the business plan, and piloted the idea, the group is ready to launch its project. The team will need to work on a marketing strategy to increase awareness about the idea. Innovators need to know their users, or customers, and how they communicate. Do they use the Internet? Do they socialize in specific places? Would it be art, photos, performances, newsletters, flyers, posts, or something else to get the users' attention? Innovators begin to gather information to tell the story of the project.

As they move forward, innovators remember to stay open to new ideas that might emerge. They remember the importance of beginner's mind. They continue to ask questions as they know that there is always more to learn.

# INTO THE FUTURE

Three years ago, Angela Zhang, a high school senior, won the Siemens Competition in Math, Science & Technology. She was curious about cancer treatments. In the announcement of her award on the Siemens website, Angela was quoted describing why she enjoyed her project. She said that it allowed her "to transform my interests in physics, chemistry, and biology into solutions for current health problems." She worked closely with a mentor from a local university and was awarded top prize.

Innovators know that creative thinking and action can happen at any time. They use their experiences to act as catalysts for change.

The ideas taught in classrooms can be enriched by experiences in the community. These work experiences can be internships, summer jobs, temporary project work, fellowships, or volunteer positions. Some opportunities may lead to future careers, and some may not. According to the National Collaborative on Workforce and Disability/Youth, paid and unpaid work experiences can teach work readiness skills and help students build their résumés. They can also foster an understanding about the demands of specific jobs and careers.

For example, students with an interest in science may work in a laboratory or research center. As interns, they might play a small role in an exciting new project. They can write about their participation on their résumés, and it can build their confidence as scientists. They may or may not be paid, but the value of the experience is great.

Innovators also look for opportunities to shine. Awards, competitions, and design challenges may provide the guidelines and resources for trying out new ideas. Many companies are offering online contests to challenge students. The experience of

After winning her award, Angela Zhang continued to innovate. She cocreated Labs on Wheels, a new project designed to make laboratory equipment accessible to all high school students and teachers.

# GETTING INSPIRED

Orville and Wilbur Wright were determined to fly, and they created many airplane prototypes to reach their goal. They endured numerous crashes and frustrations during the span of four years. They changed their designs and prototyped again and again, until they finally succeeded. The Wright brothers created the first controlled flight. The steering mechanisms they imagined in 1903 are still in use today in our modern planes.

The story of these two brothers and their adventure is told year after year in schools across America. Teachers talk about them in classrooms. Students read about them in their textbooks, on their iPads, or in the library. Their story is compelling. They had a dream to do something that people thought could never be done, and they did it.

going through the innovation process teaches young innovators many lessons before they transition from school to the workplace.

Adam Noble, eighteen, of Lakefield, Ontario, understands the process. He was recently awarded the 2013 Weston Youth Innovation Award. Adam was curious about water pollution. He was really interested in finding out how an ingredient in cosmetics, detergents, and textiles affected the water supply. After numerous tests on wastewater, Adam discovered a single-celled organism could detect and retrieve the pollutant from the water. Adam spent hundreds of hours in the lab. He built a prototype bio filter. Adam was recently quoted on the Science Centre website as saying, "My research project has grown and developed in ways that I never could have imagined."

Orville and Wilbur Wright were bold and creative, passionate about their dream, and unafraid to fail. As you read this, there are things that people believe will never happen—a cure for cancer, an end to poverty, world peace.

What are the things that you believe are impossible? What are the things that you believe are possible? What do you think will change? Look for your inspiration in the lives of innovators across history. Look for your inspiration from the lives of people in your community or in your school. Look for your inspiration in how you see the problems, challenges, or opportunities. If you have an idea, do something about it. Take that first step.

# GLOSSARY

**agenda** A list of topics that the participants in a meeting will discuss.

**analogous research** Approach to research in which students study situations that are not directly related but may allow learning opportunities related to the topic.

**associations** In innovation, the kinds of connections that people make between individuals, groups, or organizations to move an idea forward.

**business plan** A plan that describes how an idea will work.

**collaboratively** To work in partnership or together with other groups or individuals, sharing resources and expertise.

**collaborative problem solving** An approach that groups or individuals take when working together on an issue.

**customer** The user of a product, service, or outcome.

**dissuade** The opposite of persuade; to convince someone not to try to do something.

**executive functioning** A set of mental processes that allow the thinker to remember, connect, organize, and plan.

**facilitator** The leader in charge of a group.

**grant** Funding that is available to innovators for a specific purpose or goal.

**incentive** In business, something that is intended to make customers want to buy a product or service, such as discount cards, coupons, and recognition.

**iterate** To repeat after an initial attempt or test.

**launch** In business, a term describing when a group is ready to introduce a new idea to a large number of people.

**marketing strategy** In business, a term describing when a group plans how it will reach out to customers.

**mind-set** The established values, intentions, or attitudes that a person holds.

**offer** The product, service, or outcome that customers will be receiving or buying.

**prolific** Many; abundant or appearing in great numbers.

**revenue** The money that will come into a project's budget.

**touch point** A time when customers come in contact with an idea, service, or product.

Ashoka Youth Venture
Youth Venture National
1700 North Moore Street
Arlington, VA 22209
(703) 527-4126
Website: https://www.youthventure.org
Ashoka Youth Venture is part of an international network. Youth
     Venture provides support, guidance, resources, and intern-
     ship opportunities for young people who are launching or
     leading their own social innovation efforts.

Canadian Youth Business Foundation
National Office
133 Richmond Street West, Suite 700
Toronto, ON M5H 2L3
Canada
(866) 646 2922
Website: http://www.cybf.ca
This program in Canada offers mentors, training, resources, and
     seed money to young people wanting to start innovative new
     businesses.

DECA
1908 Association Drive
Reston, VA 20191
(703) 860-5000
Website: http://www.deca.org
DECA prepares emerging leaders and entrepreneurs for careers in
     marketing, finance, hospitality, and management in high

schools and colleges around the globe. DECA places value on competence, innovation, integrity, and teamwork.

d.school
Hasso Plattner Institute of Design
416 Escondido Mall
Building 550, Room 169
Stanford, CA 94305-3086
(650) 736-1025
Website: http://dschool.stanford.edu
The d.school is part of Stanford University, created to prepare future innovators. The site has manuals, videos, workshops, and more to help with human-centered design.

generationOn
281 Park Avenue South, 6th Floor
New York, NY 10010
(917) 746-8182
Website: http://www.generationon.org
This volunteer service organization challenges kids, teens, families, schools, and communities to make a difference in the world and offers tools, videos, tips, inspiration, and exciting leadership and funding opportunities.

SCORE (Service Corps of Retired Executives)
(800) 634-0245
Website: http://www.score.org
SCORE is a nationwide program that helps to connect business management counselors with innovators. SCORE has nearly 350 sites and thousands of volunteers ready to assist young people.

Social Innovation Generation
University of Waterloo
School of Environment Enterprise and Development (SEED)
Environment 3 (EV3)
200 University Avenue West
Waterloo, ON  N2L 3G1
Canada
(519) 888-4490
Website: http://www.sigeneration.ca
Social Innovation Generation (SiG) is a national partnership in
     Canada. The focus is supporting innovators of all ages as
     they respond to growing social and environmental
     challenges.

## WEBSITES

Due to the changing nature of Internet links, Rosen Publishing
has developed an online list of websites related to the subject of
this book. This site is updated regularly. Please use this link to
access the list:

http://www.rosenlinks.com/WAWR/Innov

# FOR FURTHER READING

Bassey, Nelson David, Rajasvaran Logeswaran, and Sarah Michel. *The New Generation of Leaders*. Bloomington, IN: West Bow Press, 2013.

Boss, Suzie. *Bringing Innovation to the Schools: Empowering Students to Thrive in a Changing World*. Bloomington, IN: Solution Tree Press, 2012.

The Editors at JIST. *The Young Person's Occupational Outlook Handbook*. Indianapolis, IN: JIST Publishing, 2010.

Gladwell, Malcolm. *Outliers: The Story of Success*. New York, NY: Little, Brown and Co., 2008.

Hoose, Phillip M. *We Were There, Too!: Young People in U.S. History*. New York, NY: Farrar, Straus and Giroux (BYR), 2001.

Iacoboni, Marco. *Mirroring People: The New Science of How We Connect with Others*. New York, NY: Farrar, Straus and Giroux, 2009.

Johnson, Steven. *Where Good Ideas Come From: The Natural History of Innovation*. New York, NY: Riverhead Books, 2010.

Kahnweiler, Jennifer B. *Quiet Influence: The Introvert's Guide to Making a Difference*. San Francisco, CA: Berrett-Koehler Publishers, 2013.

Kelley, Tom, and David Kelley. *Creative Confidence: Unleashing the Creative Potential Within Us All*. New York, NY: Crown Business, 2013.

Kelsey, Dee, and Pam Plumb. *Great Meetings! Great Results: A Practical Guide for Facilitating Successful, Productive Meetings*. Portland, ME: Hanson Park Press, 2004.

Lewis, Barbara. *The Teen Guide to Global Action: How to Connect with Others (Near & Far) to Create Social Change*. Minneapolis, MN: Free Spirit Publishing, 2008.

Nathan, Linda F. *The Hardest Questions Aren't on the Test: Lessons from an Innovative Urban School*. Boston, MA: Beacon Press, 2009.

Ness, Roberta. *Innovation Generation: How to Produce Creative and Useful Ideas*. New York, NY: Oxford University Press, 2012.

Paley, Steven J. *The Art of Invention: The Creative Process of Discovery and Design*. Amherst, NY: Prometheus Books, 2010.

Robinson, Ken. *Out of Our Minds: Learning to Be Creative*. Oxford, England: Capstone, 2011.

Sayer, Melissa. *Making a Difference: The Changing the World Handbook*. Ontario, Canada: Crabtree Publishing Company, 2009.

Van Wulfen, Gijs. *The Innovation Expedition: A Visual Toolkit to Start Innovation*. Amsterdam, the Netherlands: BIS Publishers, 2013.

Weinschenk, Susan. *How to Get People to Do Stuff: Master the Art and Science of Persuasion and Motivation*. Berkeley, CA: New Riders, 2013.

Ziolkowski, Jim. *Walk in Their Shoes: Can One Person Change the World?* New York, NY: Simon & Schuster, 2013.

Barnett, Chance. "Top 10 Crowdfunding Sites for Fundraising." March 8, 2013. Retrieved November 30, 2013 (http://www.forbes.com/sites/chancebarnett/2013/05/08/top-10-crowdfunding-sites-for-fundraising).

Birt, Nate. "Clayton's Bernstein Siblings Launch National Youth Volunteerism Website" March 16, 2012. Retrieved September 17, 2013 (http://clayton-richmondheights.patch.com/groups/schools/p/clayton-s-bernstein-siblings-launch-national-youth-vo939bcfa995).

Bundles, A'Lelia Perry. *On Her Own Ground: The Life and Times of Madam C.J. Walker.* New York, NY: Scribner, 2001.

Carson, Shelley. *Your Creative Brain: Seven Steps to Maximize Imagination, Productivity, and Innovation in Your Life.* San Francisco, CA: Jossey-Bass, 2010.

CBS. "How to Design Breakthrough Inventions." An interview with David Kelley, IDEO. *60 Minutes.* Aired January 6, 2013. Retrieved November 15, 2013 (http://www.cbsnews.com/videos/how-to-design-breakthrough-inventions-50138327).

Howard, Caroline. "30 Under 30: Meet the Innovators, Disrupters and Brightest Stars of 2013." December 17, 2012. Retrieved August 15, 2013 (http://www.forbes.com/sites/carolinehoward/2012/12/17/30-under-30-meet-the-innovators-disruptors-and-brightest-stars-of-2012)

Innovation Generation. "Creating More Energy." September 6, 2012. Retrieved August 28, 2013 (http://www.innovationgeneration.org/?s=&x=5&y=11).

Johnson, Sarah. "Teen Innovator Asks 'Wouldn't It Be Cool If...'"
    Retrieved December 10, 2013 (http://www.fahrenheit-212.com/
    teen-asks-wouldnt-it-be-cool-if).
National Inventors Hall of Fame. "Beulah Louise Henry."
    Retrieved November 30, 2013 (http://www.invent.org/
    hall_of_fame/273.html).
Nussbaum, Bruce. *Creative Intelligence: Harnessing the Power
    to Create, Connect, and Inspire.* New York, NY:
    HarperCollins, 2013.
Online College. "50 Famously Successful People Who Failed at
    First." February 16, 2010. Retrieved December 10, 2013
    (http://www.onlinecollege.org/2010/02/16/
    50-famously-successful-people-who-failed-at-first).
Ontario Science Centre. "Ingenious Bio Filter Earns Ontario Teen
    the 2013 Weston Youth Innovation Award." Retrieved
    November 30, 2013  (http://www.ontariosciencecentre.ca/
    Media/Details/364).
Pak, Samantha. "Charchenko: The Overlake School's 'weather-
    man.'" *Redmond Reporter*, March 23, 2012. Retrieved
    October 3, 2013 (http://www.redmond-reporter.com/
    community/143989836.html).
Ramachandranmay, Vignesh. "Teen Invents Concussion
    Detection Prototype for Car Accidents." May 14, 2013.
    Retrieved December 8, 2013 (http://mashable.com/2013/
    05/14/hardhit-concussion-detection-car-accidents).
Russsel-Brown, Deborah. "Leaders for Change: Teen Activists Speak
    on Youth Organizing and Their High School Experience." Fall
    2010. Retrieved November 30, 2013 (http://thenotebook.org/
    fall-guide-2010/102853/leaders-change).
Rutgers University. "The Thomas Edison Papers" Updated
    February 20, 2012. Retrieved December 5, 2013 (http://
    edison.rutgers.edu/biogrphy.htm).

Suzuki, Shunryu. *Zen Mind, Beginner's Mind.* Boston, MA: Shambala, 2011.

Tough, Paul. *How Children Succeed: Grit, Curiosity, and the Hidden Power of Character.* New York, NY: First Mariner Books, 2013.

Wagner, Tony. *Creating Innovators: The Making of Young People Who Will Change the World.* New York, NY: Scribner, 2012.

# INDEX

## ABOUT THE AUTHOR

Susan Burns Chong, LMSW, has worked with teens for almost twenty years. Ms. Burns Chong is a social worker at a public alternative and special education middle and high school in Maine. The students and staff at the school have great capacity to help others, improve their communities, and learn about themselves each day. She has been studying innovation as a member of a team at her school, and she is excited to share her learning through the writing of this guide.

## PHOTO CREDITS

Cover © iStockphoto.com/GlobalStock; pp. 4–5 © Jeff Greenberg 3 of 6/Alamy; p. 7 Lightspring/Shutterstock.com; p. 11 © Elias Funez/ Modesto Bee/ZUMA Press; p. 13 Fuse/Thinkstock; pp. 16–17 Sipa/ AP Images; p. 19 Fuse/Getty Images; p. 22 Jupiterimages/Stockbyte/ Thinkstock; p. 25 © David Young-Wolff/PhotoEdit; pp. 28–29 Image Source/Getty Images; p. 31 National Oceanic and Atmospheric Administration/Department of Commerce; p. 33 Bloomberg/Getty Images; p. 34 Peter Barreras/AP Images for Dyson; p. 36 The Boston Globe/Getty Images; p. 40 Stockbyte/Thinkstock; pp. 42–43 NAN728/Shutterstock.com; pp. 44–45 AFP/Getty Images; p. 48 © Lisa Werner/Alamy; cover and interior graphic elements Artens/ Shutterstock.com (figures, urban environment), LeksusTuss/ Shuttterstock.com (abstract patterns).

Designer: Brian Garvey; Editor: Andrea Sclarow Paskoff; Photo Researcher: Amy Feinberg